London's
BEST
Brunches

London's
BEST
Brunches

Laura Herring

Photography by Alicia Taylor

Smith
Street
Books

Contents

Introduction

There's something very special about brunch. It means two important things: first, that you don't need to be up early to gulp down a cup of tea on your way out the door and secondly, that there's nowhere else you have to be for a deliciously long time.

You cannot hurry brunch. No one has ever said 'let's meet for a quick brunch', or if they have, then they're not doing it right. Brunch is something to be savoured, relaxed into, considered … and then to order another Bloody Mary while you think about your next move. Maybe it's to take a wholesome stroll along the river or to check out the latest art exhibition, or perhaps it's simply to stumble back home to your sofa.

Whichever corner of London you live in (or happen to have woken up in on Saturday morning), there is the perfect spot near you to fulfil all of your morning brunch-based requirements. From cosy little local favourites to altogether more glamorous locales for a special occasion; from brunch in the middle of a park to tables high in the sky; from a classic fry-up situation to home-cured salmon or a stack of fluffy pancakes drowning in syrup, morning cocktails, freshly roasted coffee and a rainbow of life-giving juices, London has a brunch table waiting just for you.

Here is a collection of the 50 best brunches in town for your taste buds to start exploring. I hope you enjoy them as much as I did. Quite possibly I'll see you there – I'll have a side order of bacon, please.

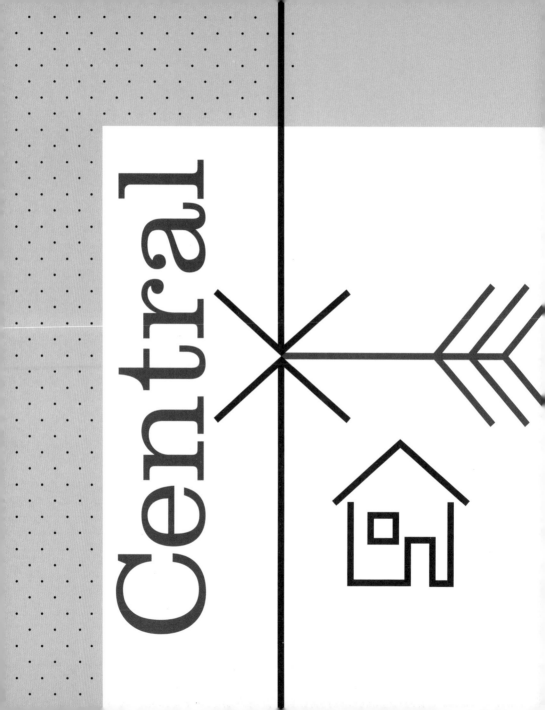

Central

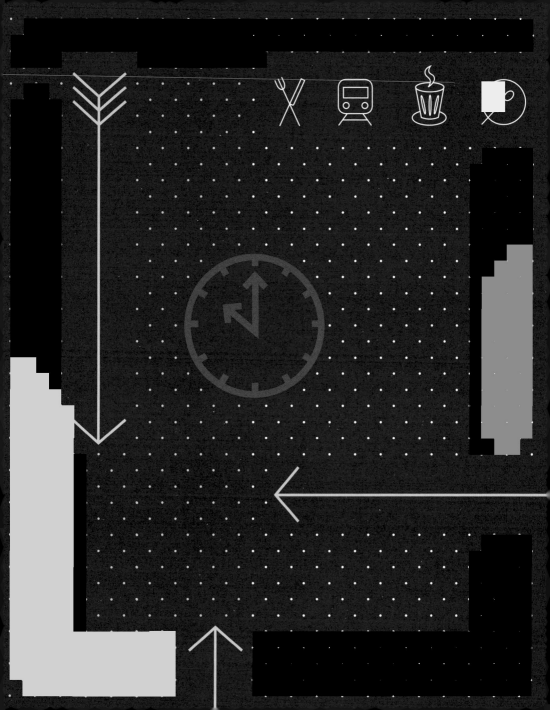

Bourne & Hollingsworth Buildings

SIGNATURE DISH: Crispy potato hash with slow braised beef

COFFEE: Nude Espresso

TEA: Mighty Leaf Tea

FOR THE MORNING AFTER: Bottomless Bellinis and Bloody Marys

 OPENING HOURS: Weekend brunch: 10am–4pm

 ADDRESS: 42 Northampton Road, EC1R 0HU

 TELEPHONE: 020 3174 1156

 NEAREST STATION: Farringdon, Angel or King's Cross

THIS IS WHERE BRUNCH TAKES IT UP A NOTCH OR TWO. A COSY café and sleek bar area opens out onto a lavish greenhouse-cum-conservatory where trailing ferns and mini palm trees provide a rather other worldly atmosphere. Wrought iron garden furniture and big comfy basket chairs mix together giving the overall impression that you've just come down to breakfast in your very rich best friend's country manor. But remember you are still in Clerkenwell, and everyone is very cool and very hip.

Enjoy a perfect cocktail while you peruse the menu, which is mainly a grown-up selection of very English dishes with a touch of adventure: curried cauliflower with a hen's egg, and huevos beneditos – a chorizo, avocado and béarnaise sauce mash-up. The house Breakfast is two eggs cooked to your liking, which you can then mix-and-match with your favourite items from a long list of classics – although it's pretty tricky not to just go for one of everything. Having said that, the crispy potato hash with braised beef is hard to beat. They also do hot drop scones and crumpets.

Stay all day enjoying the bottomless Bloody Marys.

10

Brunch in
your rich
mate's house

11

Chiltern Firehouse

SIGNATURE DISH: Lobster and crab omelette

COFFEE: Allpress

TEA: Rare Tea Company

FOR THE MORNING AFTER: An NY Classic or London Spice Bloody Mary, or a peach–apricot or hibiscus–strawberry Champagne cocktail

 OPENING HOURS: Weekend brunch: 11am–3pm

 ADDRESS: 1 Chiltern Street, W1U 7PA

 TELEPHONE: 020 7073 7676

 NEAREST STATION: Baker Street or Bond Street

SET IN AN OLD FIRE STATION, WHERE THE FIRE ENGINES USED to be parked, this has been the dining hotspot to talk about for a while now. Brunch is a bit more relaxed than dinner, but your restaurant companions are still the same perfectly groomed, rich glossy people with better hair than you. Don't think about shuffling in off the street in last night's clothes to order a bacon bap. Although since you had to book a table well ahead (and getting one is more-than-tricky), that scenario would never happen.

There are lots of little nooks to nestle into, and you can watch the chefs at work in the kitchen producing some really excellent food. The waiting staff is faultless – and there are loads of them so you feel well attended to – it's like having your own personal butlers.

The food is American-meets-European, and is mostly with a nod to healthy – which is maybe how everyone stays so skinny and polished – including oysters, crab-stuffed doughnuts (OK, maybe they're not that healthy, but they're only small), seared salmon with heritage beetroot, lobster omelettes and black-truffle scrambled eggs; and a choice between a London or NYC Bloody Mary, or Champagne cocktails.

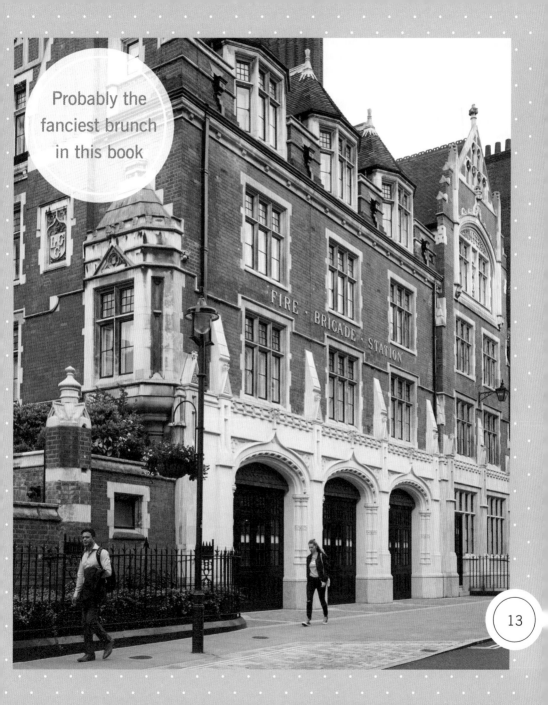

Probably the fanciest brunch in this book

FIRE · BRIGADE · STATION

13

Honey
& Co.

SIGNATURE DISH: Shakshuka

COFFEE: Cooked cardamom black

TEA: Fresh mint, rose and cinnamon, Persian lemon and fennel, plus the regulars

FOR THE MORNING AFTER: Extra merguez sausages on the side

 **OPENING HOURS:** Monday–Friday 8am–10.30pm; Saturday 9.30am–10.30pm

ADDRESS: 25a Warren Street, W1T 5LZ

TELEPHONE: 020 7388 6175

NEAREST STATION: Warren Street

THERE'S A GOOD SHORTER WEEKDAY BREAKFAST SELECTION but the weekend's Big Breakfast menu is what brunch is all about at Honey & Co. As well as Middle Eastern meets European treats – merguez sausage rolls, frittatas and a fantastic display of sweet cakes and bakes in the window – you can also enjoy figs with honey and pistachios, a heart-warming bowl of shakshuka, *green* shakshuka (with spinach), or roasted aubergines with a dinosaur egg! That's right: a dinosaur egg! Need I say more?

It's cosy inside with not a huge amount of room to move about, making this definitely not the hang-out for big noisy crowds, but it's wonderfully comforting and reassuring, and you can imagine that this is just the kind of food that the husband and wife team behind this ingenious little café enjoy at home. There are beautiful tiles on the floor for you to covet, and produce to buy on the shelves so you can take home some of the magic. On a sunny day, if you're lucky, you can sit at one of the little tables outside and pretend you're somewhere far away and not 30 seconds from the Euston Road.

The best
place to eat
dinosaur eggs

Ivy Market Grill

SIGNATURE DISH: Buttermilk pancakes or a toasted truffle chicken sandwich, depending on your mood

COFFEE: Order a pot with cream

TEA: Usuals, plus something called gunpowder tea

FOR THE MORNING AFTER: Sloe Gin Champagne Royale

OPENING HOURS: Weekend brunch: 8am–4pm

ADDRESS: 1 Henrietta Street, WC2E 8PS

TELEPHONE: 020 3301 0200

NEAREST STATION: Covent Garden

IT'S EASIER TO GET IN HERE THAN THE IVY, BUT THAT'S NOT the only reason to go. Like its bigger sibling, the atmosphere here feels a little bit buzzy and there are plenty of people to half-recognise and side-glance at over your Market Grill Bloody Mary or Salted Caramel Espresso Martini. The décor is old New York meets Paris in its glory days – leather booths, a zinc bar top, polished wood, beautiful tiles on the floor and impressive floor-to-ceiling windows.

The brunch menu is a bit overwhelming: a large page of small type listing basically anything you can think of – mostly with a bit of added luxury: lobster benedict, truffled scrambled eggs, yoghurt and berries with bee pollen on top. From toast and jam to a 12-oz grain-fed Argentinian rib-eye with parmesan chips, every hunger can be sated, and all with a discreet smile from your friendly waiter. There is also a good selection of desserts. This isn't The Ivy, so don't expect it to be, but it makes a nice change from a greasy spoon.

A
laid-back
little brother

17

Kopapa

SIGNATURE DISH: Turkish eggs with whipped yoghurt and chilli butter

COFFEE: Kopapa Blend roasted exclusively by the Monmouth Coffee Company

TEA: In pots large enough for 2 cups

FOR THE MORNING AFTER: Orchard Fizz: apples, pears, vodka and prosecco

 OPENING HOURS: Weekend brunch: 9.30am–4.30pm

 ADDRESS: 32–34 Monmouth Street, WC2H 9HA

 TELEPHONE: 020 7240 6076

 NEAREST STATION: Covent Garden or Leicester Square

ON THEIR WEBSITE IT SAYS THAT 'KOPAPA' IS A MAORI WORD that means 'a gathering, to be crowded, and a building to store food in'. Kopapa is all of these things. It is the perfect place to gather because of its excellent central location in Seven Dials in Covent Garden, and also because of its top-notch grub. I don't know about how they store their food, but I can tell you that it's pretty delicious on a plate. But both of these things also means it does tend to get very crowded at the weekends, so it's not a place you can linger leisurely; it's a place to meet and catch up before going on somewhere else – to browse the shops, visit a gallery or wander around the old streets of London.

The chefs behind this West End venture are predominantly of New Zealand heritage – so the coffee is excellent, and they do a mean avo' on toast. The weekend-only brunch menu includes Turkish eggs and chorizo hash, and is definitely worth checking out. Each of the dairy-free smoothies come with an ingredient you can't quite pronounce, so they must be good for you – but you can balance this out perfectly with a crème brûlée doughnut.

18

Antipodean
meets Middle
Eastern in the
West End

Roast

SIGNATURE DISH: The Full Borough

COFFEE: Roast special blend, plus others

TEA: Roast special tea blend, plus a great selection including Pu-erh 10 Year's Old

FOR THE MORNING AFTER: Bubbles, obviously

 **OPENING HOURS:** Breakfast: Monday–Friday 7am–11am; Saturday 8.30am–11.30am

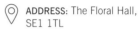 **ADDRESS:** The Floral Hall, SE1 1TL

TELEPHONE: 020 3006 6111

 **NEAREST STATION:** London Bridge

ROAST OFFERS UP A SLIGHTLY MORE FORMAL, STARCHED-white-tablecloth kind of brunch experience, set in a large airy dining room with big windows overlooking Borough Market and the busy surrounding side streets. Everything has a clean and neat finish – even the waiting staff are in uniform – and the food is very precise on the plate. Don't be surprised to see shirts and ties worn to breakfast. But, having said all of that, it still manages to have a relaxed atmosphere congenial to a good slap-up meal.

Many of the ingredients are sourced from the famous market below, and the restaurant prides itself on its very British produce. It is a seasonal and changing menu, but the stalwarts remain: The Full Borough – a more than acceptable fry-up – The Full Scottish, with haggis and a tattie scone, and The Veggie Borough. There's also trout, kippers, smoked haddock and granuesli (granola meets muesli in case you weren't sure). Or else you can keep it simple with a boiled egg and Marmite soldiers.

Smart dining above London's famous Borough Market

The Lockhart

SIGNATURE DISH: Fried chicken and waffles with maple syrup

COFFEE: Union

TEA: Rare Tea

FOR THE MORNING AFTER: Bottomless coffee

OPENING HOURS: Weekend brunch: 11am–3pm

ADDRESS: 22–24 Seymour Place, W1H 7NL

TELEPHONE: 0203 011 5400

NEAREST STATION: Marble Arch

IF YOU'RE JUST AFTER A LIGHT BOWL OF YOGHURT AND FRUIT, then this maybe isn't the place for you (although there is a token healthy option on the menu in the form of maple pecan granola). No; here is where you come to live out your American food dream and learn, once and for all, what corn grits are and how they should actually always be cooked with shrimps, while discussing how different a US 'biscuit' really is from a UK scone – and why it's perfectly OK to serve them covered in sausage gravy at breakfast.

The chef behind this mastery hails from Mississippi via Brooklyn ending up in Marylebone, and that's exactly the kind of food you'll be enjoying. Fried chicken and waffles with a bucket of maple syrup, candied pork jowl and scrambled eggs, or ribs and 'slaw – but all cleanly served in a bright, light two-storey dining room. Old railway benches and carefully chosen vintage furniture give a relaxed feel to the whole experience. But make no mistake: this is properly well done food.

After your Southern States feast you can take a stroll round the very English Hyde Park and maybe pop over to The Palace to regain your Britishness.

Mississippi
meets
Marylebone

The Modern Pantry

SIGNATURE DISH: Tea-smoked salmon on an English muffin with yuzu hollandaise and hazelnut and macadamia dukka

COFFEE: Caravan Coffee Roasters

TEA: Newby Teas, and mint iced tea

FOR THE MORNING AFTER: Japanese Mary

 OPENING HOURS: Weekend brunch: Saturday 9am–4pm; Sunday 10am–4pm

 ADDRESS: 47–48 St John's Square, EC1V 4JJ

TELEPHONE: 020 7553 9210

NEAREST STATION: Farringdon

THERE'S SOMETHING ABOUT THE MODERN PANTRY THAT MAKES you want to hide your hangover. Or, at least, not let it overtake you, because from its charming setting in a Grade II listed townhouse on St. John's Square – whether you're sitting outside in the sunshine or letting the light come in through the big sash windows – to its relaxed and welcoming atmosphere, it feels like you've been invited into someone very lovely's home and you want to make a good impression. There's just too much to enjoy here to even contemplate a headache. And that's before you even get to the food.

The menu has all you'd expect from an English brunch, but everything has a little twist or tasty surprise to get you excited. The salmon is tea-smoked, the hollandaise is subtly flavoured with yuzu, the chips are cassava, and the chicken burger is Persian and comes with coconut and black sesame labneh. You'll want to keep ordering the extras, snacks and small plates just to find out which is your favourite. And I'd recommend a house hot chocolate if you have any room left – classic, liquorice and chilli, or malt and caraway. They are a little bit rich but also exactly what you needed without knowing it.

Relaxed, quirky flavours in a very English setting

The Table

SIGNATURE DISH: The Stack: chorizo, ham hock baked beans, poached eggs and hollandaise on a bagel

COFFEE: Allpress

TEA: Tea Pig

FOR THE MORNING AFTER: A cold-pressed juice from the Neat Juicery or Gosnells Mead from Peckham

 OPENING HOURS: Weekend brunch: 8.30am–4.30pm

 ADDRESS: 83 Southwark Street, SE1 0HX

 TELEPHONE: 0207 401 2760

 NEAREST STATION: Southwark

BRILLIANTLY LOCATED A BRIEF STROLL FROM TATE MODERN, this is the perfect place to refuel after your weekend art fix before mooching back along the South Bank. Big tables with long benches to sit on and a garden area – well, a generous backyard for when it's warmer weather – means there's ample room to sprawl and enjoy the menu.

The Table is a well-oiled machine, but don't be fooled by its sleek exterior, as this is a café with ethics. Food is sourced from suppliers who can ensure sustainability and the kitchen supports the local homeless charity St Mungo's, who supply herbs and salads and all sorts of goodies from their allotments.

The Borough Full English is not to be missed: bacon on the right side of crispy and homemade baked beans are a highlight. And there's a Vegetarian Borough with buttery spinach and haloumi. But if you're feeling on the hangry side, then The Stack is the choice for you – chorizo and ham hock baked beans on a bagel with poached eggs and hollandaise; it is, as they quite rightly say on their menu, a 'towering inferno of deliciousness'. The sweetcorn fritters offer a lighter, but equally well-thought out option, and the buttermilk pancakes and waffles come with an imaginative selection of toppings.

Sustainable food just off the South Bank

Workshop Coffee Co.

SIGNATURE DISH: Full Benedict: English muffin, ham hock, poached eggs, spinach, chipotle sauce

COFFEE: Beans carefully sourced from around the world

TEA: Waterloo Tea

FOR THE MORNING AFTER: Rosy Mimosa

   OPENING HOURS: Weekend brunch: Saturday and Sunday 8:00am–6:00pm

ADDRESS: 27 Clerkenwell Road, EC1M 5RN

TELEPHONE: 0207 253 5754

NEAREST STATION: Farringdon or Barbican

THE TEAM BEHIND THE WORKSHOP COFFEE CO. ARE A BIT obsessed with getting the best possible coffee into your cup. They travel the world and bring back their favourite beans and then roast them to perfection. The actual choice on the menu is surprisingly brief, but you can be sure that it has been thoroughly tested against their strict quality control – and will have passed with flying colours. Coffee is serious business.

With exposed brick walls, polished wooden floors and an industrial/canteen décor you can expect lots of bearded, tattooed, hipster expert-baristas to serve you your weekend brunch. The menu has a bit of an international feel with huevos rancheros sitting happily alongside morcilla sausages and chorizo baked eggs. If you're in the mood for sharing, order some ricotta waffles with spectacularly smoky bacon for the table, or frittata with mini corn muffins. There are also some lighter options – granola, poached fruit, porridge – if you're feeling a bit more wholesome.

Brunch here is busy and noisy. I'm not sure it's quite the place to linger and while away the hours on a lazy Sunday, but it will get you going for the rest of the day. Even if that's just meandering home to the sofa.

Coffee with
a conscience

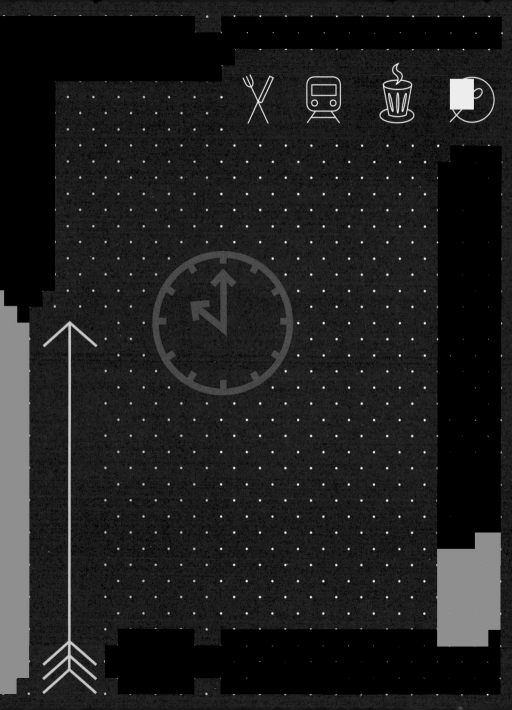

Boulangerie Bon Matin

SIGNATURE DISH: Pastries and bread straight from their ovens

COFFEE: Excellent, just as you'd expect from France

TEA: English breakfast, Earl Grey or Assam, or a selection of herbals

FOR THE MORNING AFTER: Fresh juices and smoothies made on request

 OPENING HOURS: 7am–6.30pm

 ADDRESS: 178 Tollington Park, N4 3AJ

TELEPHONE: 020 7263 8633

 NEAREST STATION: Finsbury Park

YOU CAN SMELL THE FRESHLY BAKED BREADS AND PÂTISSERIE from down the road, before you can even see the piles of cakes in the window. This is a little taste of bon Français on a busy London street. The brunch menu is predominantly vegetarian, with a good selection of egg-based dishes, and a full-plate veggie breakfast which includes deliciously hot rosemary potatoes. But what you've really come for are the pastries, and they don't disappoint. Of course, for the complete French experience, you shouldn't miss out on a crepe either – both sweet and savoury filling options are available – and the French toast is made from their own brioche and is definitely worth the trip up Tolly Park Road.

There is seating on stools in the window, if you're just passing through for a cup of coffee and a fresh-from-the-oven croissant or pain au chocolat, but if you're in for a longer stay, the back room has tables and lots of light through the ceiling windows. Perfect for reading the free weekend papers. *C'est un bon weekend.*

A French
village bakery
in Finsbury
Park

33

Caravan

SIGNATURE DISH: Baked eggs with merguez sausage

COFFEE: Single-estate, lovingly sourced

TEA: Yes, all kinds

FOR THE MORNING AFTER: A well-stocked bar

 OPENING HOURS: Weekend brunch: 10am–4pm

 ADDRESS: 1 Granary Building, Granary Square, N1C 4AA

 TELEPHONE: 020 7101 7661

 NEAREST STATION: King's Cross

WITH A LONG MENU THAT INCLUDES SIDES AND PUDDING, YOU could easily stay at Caravan for the whole brunch service – from 10am–4pm – eating your way through the list. The fry-ups (with optional add-ons of chorizo or wild boar sausages) are superb, but it would be a shame not to try some of the more unusual listings while you're there. Coconut bread with fruit, or the pumpkin waffles with ricotta and maple syrup are just the right side of sweet, while their homemade jalapeño corn bread with chilli jam and feta will leave you feeling satisfied and ready for a day of wholesome activity. If you can handle something a bit richer and don't have to be anywhere for a while (giving you plenty of time to digest), the kimchi pancakes with pork belly, duck egg and sweet and smoky crème fraîche will give your taste buds a treat.

Wooden tables are crammed inside a big, high-ceilinged room with a bit of an industrial feel. It can get busy and you sometimes have to shout over the noise of other diners so if you're going *à deux*, aim for a corner – or, even better, a window seat so you can keep an eye on the fountains outside. Coffee is a priority at Caravan, and beans are sourced from single estates around the world and roasted on-site. And if you like it that much, you can even buy some beans to take home.

Not your average eggs and bacon

Duke's Brew & Que

SIGNATURE DISH:
The Breakfast Burger

COFFEE: Caravan, but it's more about the craft beers

TEA: Earl Grey, builders' and all the regulars

FOR THE MORNING AFTER: Bloody Marys, of course, or beer from local Beavertown Brewery

 OPENING HOURS: Weekend lunch menu: 12pm–4pm

 ADDRESS: 33 Downham Road, N1 5AA

 TELEPHONE: 020 3006 0795

 NEAREST STATION: Haggerston

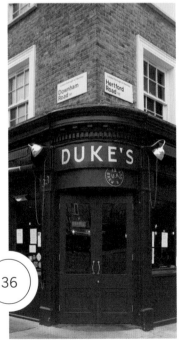

WITH A BIG AMERICAN-STYLE GRILL IN THE KITCHEN, everything here has a smoky, deep-South twang. If this is really what the lucky folk in the Southern States eat every day, then they must be laughing mightily hard at our boiled eggs and soldiers.

The weekend menu is a reduced version of the regular weekday dinner treats: hunks of sweet, juicy meat in the form of beautifully messy pork and beef ribs that will kick any hangover out of the ballpark. It may seem strange and tug at your English reserve to be eating chunks of beef so early in the morning, with rib sauce all over your face, but you'll soon get over any hesitations once you sink your teeth into all that goodness. If you thought ribs for breakfast were too much, then the Breakfast Burger is out of control – a teetering stack of meaty heaven topped with an egg that is trying, but failing, to be trapped inside a bun. If you're after something a bit sweeter, Mr Frenchie and his Ravioli save the day. It's a feast of French toast stuffed with bacon and cream cheese – again, it might sound a bit much, but it really isn't.

The staff are friendly, the vibe is laid-back, and the beer menu changes regularly so you can sample all the craft beers you can handle.

To banish
a hangover

Fink's Salt and Sweet

SIGNATURE DISH: Salmon from the House of Sverre

COFFEE: Caravan Market blend

TEA: All the usuals

FOR THE MORNING AFTER: Pickle Mary: Bloody Mary with a sharp shot of pickle juice

 OPENING HOURS: Weekend brunch: Saturday 9am–5pm; Sunday 8am–5pm

 ADDRESS: 70 Mountgrove Road, N5 2LT

TELEPHONE: 020 7684 7189

 NEAREST STATION: Finsbury Park or Arsenal

THIS IS A PLACE FOR THE COOL YOUNG THINGS. POSITIONED ON the corner on the site of a Victorian butcher's, the beautiful floor-to-ceiling windows flood the room with light. It's noisy with the chatter of interesting people talking about interesting things over good coffee and even better food. On a warm day you can sit at one of their ten coveted outside seats.

One thing not to miss is the smoked salmon. It literally glows with a rich, orange light, luring you, like a greedy moth into its oily deliciousness. It is smoked just around the corner and delivered fresh to the deli. And what a deli. They describe it as 'your fridge, only better'. And that's exactly right; it's just what you would wish those bare shelves of yours to heave with: local cheese, English hams, creamy burrata, the famous E17 Walthamstow bacon jam, fresh pesto, charcuterie and delicious sourdough bread. And the challah bread cinnamon toast (with or without bacon) and great selection of cakes that always adorn the counter will please those with a sweet tooth.

To sort out any lingering cobwebs, order a Pickle Mary, with its deliciously sour taste of pickle juice (which you can buy in bottles to take home) and crunchy cornichon garnish.

Scandi cool with an enviable deli

Foxlow

SIGNATURE DISH: Fried chicken and croissant waffle

COFFEE: Union Roasters

TEA: Rare Tea Company

FOR THE MORNING AFTER: Smokestack Mary: gin, chipotle and smoked paprika or the Foxlow Mimosa or the Bottomless Bloody Mary

 OPENING HOURS: Brunch menu: weekdays 12pm–3pm; weekends 10am–3pm

 ADDRESS: 71–73 Stoke Newington Church Street, N16 0AS

 TELEPHONE: 020 7481 6377

 NEAREST STATION: Stoke Newington

THE OWNERS SAY ON THEIR WEBSITE THAT THEY OPENED Foxlow because they 'just wanted to open the kind of restaurant we would like to live near'. And I wish I lived a bit closer.

The brunch menu is quite brief but each dish is perfectly thought-out, and looks pretty on the plate too. At the lighter end of the scale is homemade ricotta and London honey with a delicate garnish of orange zest and thyme. At the other end of the greedy spectrum, you'll find their now famous fried chicken and egg croissant waffle. Now, it may sound as though you have just stepped beyond a sensible breakfast choice but somehow it works, and it resolves the age-old question what came first, the chicken or the egg? The answer is they came together on a perfectly cooked waffle boat. The Moroccan baked eggs are probably the most popular dish they serve, and if you can get over the fact you're eating steak very soon after you've woken up, you will have made an excellent food choice with the steak, eggs and fiercesome green harissa. There are plenty of sides too, including avocado, sweet potato hash and something called a flat sausage, which is exactly what it sounds like.

The quality of the produce is superb and the attention to flavour detail is expert. Although you'd expect nothing less from the team behind the Hawksmoor.

Another success from the Hawksmoor

Franks
Canteen

SIGNATURE DISH: The menu changes but poached eggs with your choice of extras is a fail-safe winner

COFFEE: Two shots, as standard

TEA: Served in large mugs

FOR THE MORNING AFTER: A Kiss on the Beach: cranberry and orange juice

 OPENING HOURS: Wednesday–Friday 9am–2.30pm; Saturday 9am–3pm; Sunday 9am–2pm (check the website or Twitter for this week's opening hours)

 ADDRESS: 86 Highbury Park, N5 2XE

 TELEPHONE: 07717 683651

 NEAREST STATION: Arsenal

THE MENU AT FRANKS IS SMALL BUT PERFECTLY FORMED, changing from time to time to keep up with the seasons, and sometimes just to keep things interesting. Breakfast is served all day, so you can relax and enjoy the sunshine streaming through the windows while sitting at one of the sturdy wooden farmhouse tables. There's space for only a chosen few so get there early if you can. The owner and chef, Paul (Frank is the name of his young son) also caters for weddings, so opening hours can be a bit erratic if he's looking after an event – but he keeps his fans updated via Twitter.

The eggs, bacon, sausages and smoked salmon are all sourced from around England, and the black pudding is particularly moreish. But when it's on the menu, it's the kedgeree that really wins out here: creamy and satisfying and perfectly spiced, the flavours are balanced to perfection. There's also a slight Middle Eastern twist to the listings with merguez sausages and hints of harissa popping up. Keep going back to see what's new to try.

So local,
it feels a bit
like your own
dining room

Greenberry Café

SIGNATURE DISH: Homemade granola with coconut yoghurt

COFFEE: Climpson & Son

TEA: Loose-leaf, just as it should be

FOR THE MORNING AFTER: A good wine list, including some fine English bottles

 OPENING HOURS: Weekend brunch: Saturday 9am–3pm; Sunday 9am–4pm

 ADDRESS: 101 Regent's Park Road, NW1 8UR

 TELEPHONE: 020 7483 3765

NEAREST STATION: Chalk Farm

THE OUTSIDE IS PAINTED A RATHER GARISH MINTY GREEN, and the big windows are scrawled with their menu, while the inside has some rather lovely bare brick walls on show. The Greenberry Café (or just The Greenberry, to those in the know) is a busy, noisy café, perfect for rubbing shoulders with – and sometimes the noses of the adorable dogs belonging to – the Primrose Hill locals.

This is a relaxed place to while away an hour or two over homemade granola or a bowl of warming shakshuka. The menu takes it lead from all over the world, which sounds like a bit of a hotchpotch, but it's all done so very well, meaning whatever you fancy eating, your needs can be met – be that a fry-up of the finest bacon and Burford Brown eggs, kedgeree or quinoa porridge. And if you hang on until 12pm, you can also choose from their lunch menu – I had my eye on a royal-looking Reuben… The owner also provides a changing selection of homemade ice creams and sorbets.

The chic way to do relaxed brunch

SUNDAY

SIGNATURE DISH: SUNDAY Full Breakfast; pancakes or courgette fritters

COFFEE: Caravan

TEA: Joe's Tea Company

FOR THE MORNING AFTER: Aperol spritzes, and keep them coming

OPENING HOURS: Tuesday and Wednesday breakfast 8.30am–6pm; Thursday and Friday breakfast 8.30am–5pm; weekend brunch 10am–5pm

ADDRESS: 169 Hemingford Road, N1 1DA

TELEPHONE: 020 7607 3868

NEAREST STATION: Caledonian Road & Barnsbury or Highbury & Islington

A GREAT LITTLE HIDEAWAY LOCAL MUCH LOVED BY ALL IN THE neighbourhood. There are always queues but once you're inside it's like you've been let into a little secret. There's a cute garden and a relaxed atmosphere as everyone is just busy getting on with the important weekend task of having a good time.

The menu is seasonal and changes often but is always based around great brunch standards, with a bit of a twist. House granola is a quinoa granola, the waffles are cornbread with a pepper ragu, and the butter on your pile of freshly cooked pancakes is honeycomb. If you can't decide between avocado on toast or a full English, maybe go for the chorizo and minced beef hash with poached egg, avocado and toast, with a corn fritter on the side – then you can basically taste everything on the menu at once. And finish up with a freshly made cake – or doughnuts! – for pudding.

SUNDAY is what Sundays (and Saturdays) are all about.

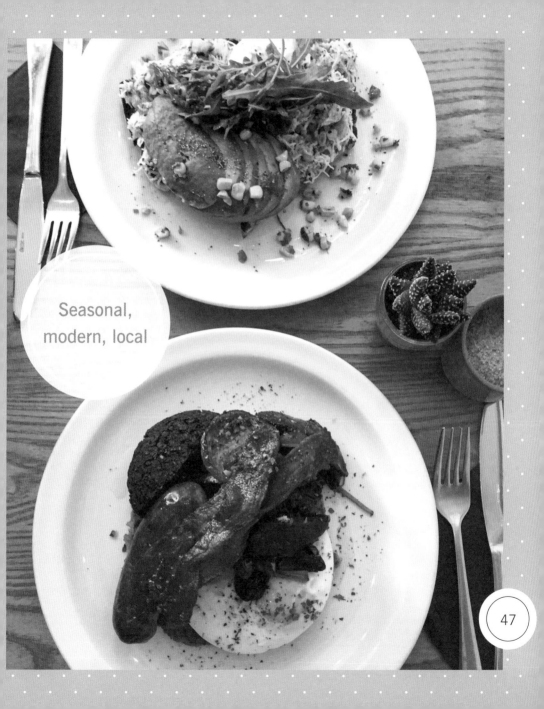

Seasonal,
modern, local

The Haberdashery

SIGNATURE DISH: Veggie Breakfast

COFFEE: Brick Lane's Nude Espresso Micro-Roastery

TEA: Loose-leaf teas from W. Martyn of Muswell Hill

FOR THE MORNING AFTER: A 'who needs yoga' fresh juice or a Beetroot Bloody Mary

  OPENING HOURS: 9am–6pm

 ADDRESS: 22 Middle Lane, N8 8PL

TELEPHONE: 020 8342 8098

 NEAREST STATION: Crouch Hill

THERE IS SOMETHING A LITTLE BIT VILLAGE FETE ABOUT The Haberdashery. Maybe it's the vintage teacups and saucers behind the counter, or the tote bags and handicrafts for sale by the till. Either way, it's a cosy, comforting place to be. And the food is top-notch too.

It gets *very* busy and there can be long waits, but if you're patient or get there early, you will be rewarded: a cooked breakfast so big it almost doesn't fit on the plate, very thick wedges of French toast, or a breakfast baguette with overflowing bacon, eggs, sausage and homemade tomato jam. There's also a 'Light Breakfasts' part of the menu including porridge with poached fruit, muesli, and a junior version of the breakfast baguette, as well as croissants, cinnamon swirls and muffins of the day.

And, in-keeping with the community feel, they also run evening events from supper clubs to vintage markets and music nights.

Also located in Stoke Newington.

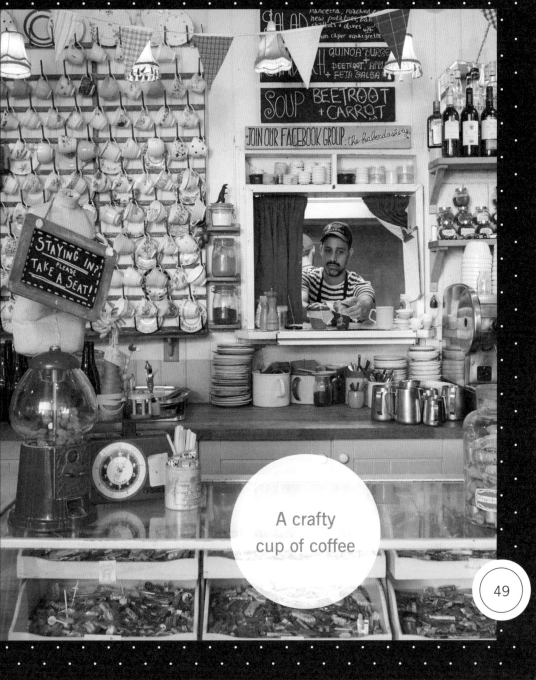

A crafty
cup of coffee

The Towpath Café

SIGNATURE DISH: Cheese toastie

COFFEE: Piansa, imported direct

TEA: The usual crowd

FOR THE MORNING AFTER: All-day gin!

OPENING HOURS: Tuesday–Friday 8am–dusk; Saturday and Sunday 9am–dusk (March to November)

ADDRESS: Regent's Canal towpath (between Whitmore Bridge and Kingsland Road Bridge), N1 5SB

TELEPHONE: 020 7254 7606

NEAREST STATION: Haggerston

SITTING RIGHT ON THE WATERSIDE OF REGENT'S CANAL IN Hackney, sun shining, blue sky, sipping some really great coffee and munching on a warm, cheese toastie (with quince paste), sometimes London feels like the best place in the world!

You can't not be in a good mood at The Towpath Café – everyone seems to know each other and, being a little out of the way, most people are locals. Lovers, families, writers, joggers, people just out for a walk along the banks of the canal – everyone is welcome. It's a bit of a squeeze and you'll be lucky to get a seat at one of the tables, and it *is* a bit weather-dependent (it's not quite so pleasant when it's raining) but if you do manage to find a corner inside, you could happily stay for brunch into lunch into dinner.

The brunch menu isn't huge, but there's something to tick every box: eggs on toast, porridge or granola, cakes at the counter, and plenty of coffee.

Just watch out for the bells from oncoming cyclists.

About
as London
as it gets

East

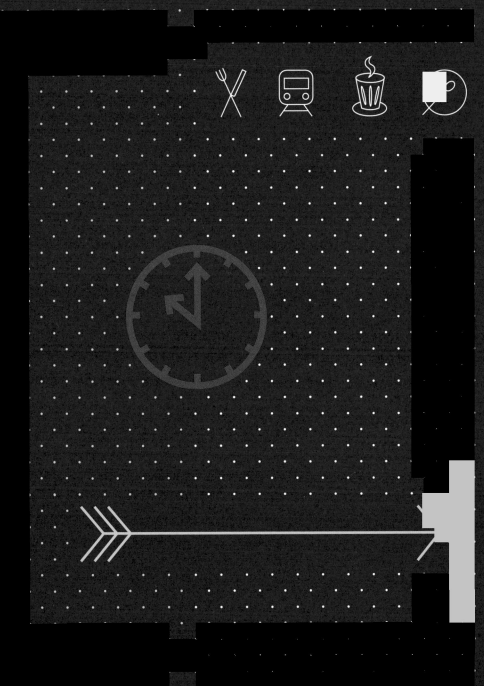

Albion
Café

SIGNATURE DISH: Full Albion Breakfast: a traditional fry-up

COFFEE: Italian brand Musetti

TEA: We Are Tea

FOR THE MORNING AFTER: A reviving Detox drink

 OPENING HOURS: Breakfast menu: Monday–Friday 8am–12pm; weekends 8am–12.30pm

 ADDRESS: 2–4 Boundary Street, E2 7DD

 TELEPHONE: 020 7729 1051

 NEAREST STATION: Shoreditch High Street

THERE IS A BIT OF AN ENGLISH VILLAGE SHOP FEEL ABOUT THE Albion. It is a café meets bakery meets grocery shop where you can enjoy your breakfast and then pick up some great British ingredients to take home for round two. The menu concentrates on traditional home-cooking with lots of good, solid hairs-on-your-chest food: a traditional fry-up, eggs every which way, sausage, egg and bacon sandwiches in any combination, and for more of an old-school morning feast, kippers or kidneys on toast or porridge with prunes. There are also some changing specials – such as the sweet potato and spinach hash.

The shop sells fresh produce from around the British Isles and with the seasons, and you can stock up your store cupboard too with everything from flour to pickles to biscuits to goose fat. Plus smoked fish, organic meats and, during certain months of the year, you can bag yourself a pheasant. Terrance Conran's kitchen garden even provides some fresh fruit and veg. The bakery sells every kind of bread and pastry you can imagine, freshly made on site – perfect big squishy bloomers, Danish pastries and sausage rolls, strawberry tarts, huge sponge cakes and festive specials. There's even an enormous, head-sized jammy dodger.

A very
British café
and local
shop

55

Andina

SIGNATURE DISH: Picante de huevos

COFFEE: Own blend

TEA: Andean mint, 100% Peruvian chamomile, among other specials

FOR THE MORNING AFTER: The Super Bloody Mary with tomato, beetroot, red pepper, cucumber and pisco infused with celery, smoked vodka and tiger's milk

 OPENING HOURS: Weekdays 8am–11am; weekend brunch 10am–4pm

 ADDRESS: 1 Redchurch Street, E2 7DJ

 TELEPHONE: 020 7920 6499

 NEAREST STATION: Shoreditch High Street

GROWING UP IN PERU, OWNER MARTIN MORALES USED TO receive care packages full of tasty goodies each month from his grandma who lived in the Andes, and now he's spreading the Andean love in Shoreditch. It's a gluten-free, dairy-free dream of quinoa, amaranth and chia seeds. Everything overflows with punchy flavours that will knock you sideways by their unexpected intensity – and many also with such a flash of fire that you'll wake up out of any dreamy Sunday daze you may be in, while simultaneously managing to keep you warm and toasty all afternoon.

Get there early so you can get a prime seat upstairs, but if you do have to squeeze into the downstairs dining room, you'll be so distracted by your food that you won't even mind not having a window seat. Poached eggs come in a rich chilli and tomato sauce; a perfectly balanced quinoa and aramanth granola is topped with berries and so many wholesome goodies you'll feel powered up and ready to go. There are lots of juices and smoothies to choose from, each one full of exotic and magical superfoods that whisper the secrets of eternal youth.

Fresh and fiery, and a real adventure for your taste buds, Andina is perfect for when you fancy a change from the reliable favourites, and may well even become a new weekend tradition.

Trust me, you need a Peruvian brunch

Beagle

SIGNATURE DISH: Buttermilk pancakes or bacon hash

COFFEE: Workshop Coffee Co.

TEA: Skip to the Bloody Mary menu

FOR THE MORNING AFTER: All of the Bloody Marys

 OPENING HOURS: Weekend brunch: Saturday 11am–3pm; Sunday 11am–2pm

 ADDRESS: 397–400 Geffrye Sreet, E2 8HZ

TELEPHONE: 020 7613 2967

NEAREST STATION: Hoxton

BARE BRICK WALLS? TICK. SET UNDER SOME OLD RAILWAY arches? Tick. Excellent and unusual cocktail menu? Tick. You must be in East London! Styled a little bit like a station café, Beagle is everything you'd expect from a Hoxton bar and restaurant. It is even named after an old steam train that used to travel the rails above it.

The menu is predominantly American–English – buttermilk pancakes with seasonal fruits, eggs and hollandaise on toasted brioche, smoked bacon hash with fried eggs, or a smoked ham and sauerkraut toastie. A Middle Eastern wild card is the goat kofte with freekeh, labneh and flatbreads – but then that's very E2. If you're feeling a bit flash you can even get some oysters to go with your morning cocktail while you wait for your main course. There are some really great drinks to choose from, although is it a bit early for bourbon? Possibly. Maybe stick to the long list of Bloody Marys. There are also lots of extras you can add-on to your plate, so you can create your own dream breakfast. And as we all know, anything is infinitely improved with duck fat chips.

A very
Hoxton
brunch

Counter Café

SIGNATURE DISH: Bacon roll with Counter relish

COFFEE: Counter Café roasted on the premises

TEA: It's really the coffee you came for

FOR THE MORNING AFTER: It's all about the strong coffee

 OPENING HOURS: Monday–Friday 7.30am–5pm; weekends 9am–5pm

ADDRESS: 7 Roach Road, E3 2PA

TELEPHONE: 07834 275920

NEAREST STATION: Hackney Wick

ON THE DECK OF THEIR SPACIOUS JETTY YOU CAN SIT BACK AND watch as other people more active than you canoe up and down the canal, with the Olympic Park as an inspirational backdrop. As your perfectly roasted and brewed cup of coffee arrives, you can nosy at the houseboats across the water. With art on the walls both inside and out, and positioned in one of the most creative hotspots in the capital, Counter Café is a step away from reality in the best possible way.

It is simple breakfast food but excellently executed, and everything that can be is homemade – from the relish in the bacon rolls to the actual sausages that are actually, truly made onsite. They also do a good line in eggs benedict, French toast, Turkish eggs, bagels and muesli. The coffee is the star here though; lovingly selected, roasted in the back, tasted and packaged up in pretty bags. And their website even lets you know how many kilos they've roasted so far that week – and how many eggs have been poached! (25 kg and 250 respectively so far and it's only Tuesday.) This is a place that is buzzing with energy and enterprise and people on the go.

A canal-side breakfast with views of the Olympic Park

61

Dishoom

SIGNATURE DISH: Naan rolls

COFFEE: Monsooned Malabar Coffee

TEA: Lightly spiced house chai

FOR THE MORNING AFTER: The Dhoble (apparently named after the Assistant Commissioner of Police in Bombay, Vasant Dhoble): gin, maraschino liqueur with orange and lemon juice

 OPENING HOURS: Monday–Friday 8am–11.30am; weekends 9am–12am

 ADDRESS: 7 Boundary Street, E2 7JE

 TELEPHONE: 020 7420 9324

 NEAREST STATION: Shoreditch High Street

THE TRADITIONAL IRANI-BOMBAY CAFÉS AFTER WHICH DISHOOM is styled were classless hubs; noisy, busy centres where everyone and anyone met and ate and worked and whiled away lots of time. London Dishoom captures some of that atmosphere as a wonderful place to relax and unwind. There are plush leather booths, marble slabs and chandeliers, but it's all a little bit tongue-in-cheek, with a laid-back feel to the whole event – and someone's brilliant Indian family portraits watching over you from the wall. There's also a charming little verandah for warmer weather – with a few games and books – so it feels a little bit like a club house.

The menu is predominantly Indian street food meets English staples. There are lots of good egg-based dishes, including keema per eedu – a 'Parsi power breakfast' of spicy chicken with fried eggs, chips and bread. But it's the naan rolls that have won Dishoom their loyal breakfasting following: sausage, bacon and eggs in various combinations wrapped in fluffy warm naan with fresh herbs. For a more serious hunger to sate, try The Big Bombay, a twist on a classic full English with marsala baked beans. At the other end of the scale, there are lighter dishes: fruit, yoghurt and house granola. Juices are made to order but a breakfast lassi is what you really need.

Brunch,
Bombay
café-style

Duck
& Waffle

SIGNATURE DISH: Duck & Waffle

COFFEE: Moschetti

TEA: Jing

FOR THE MORNING AFTER: Marmite Black Velvet: Marmite and Guinness reduction with Champagne

 OPENING HOURS: Weekend brunch: 9am–4pm

 ADDRESS: Heron Tower, 110 Bishopsgate, EC2N 4AY

 TELEPHONE: 020 3640 7310

 NEAREST STATION: Liverpool Street

THERE'S SOMETHING GIDDILY EXCITING ABOUT BEING HIGH UP in the sky, purveying a city far below. Maybe it draws on a kind of megalomania deep within us all, a kind of emperor complex – a king surveying his kingdom (or queen over her queendom). And to *eat* while balanced on top of the world, well, can it get any more thrilling? Even if you're only here for an hour for brunch, there's something quite magical about being 40 floors up above London – the highest restaurant in the UK, FYI.

The menu swings a bit wildly from Asian to American to British, via Italy and France, but it's all very delicious. And there are a few items that marry unexpected flavours: ox-cheek doughnuts, and foie gras crème brûlée being two notable examples. But when you're sitting in the clouds, anything goes. The duck egg en cocotte with roasted red peppers is rich and special enough to keep up with the view; and, of course, their signature duck (leg and egg) perched on a waffle is suitably impressive. There is a good range of sweet plates too – a peanut crunch dark chocolate sundae is quite enough sugar for the best of us. With amazing views and open 24 hours a day (although brunch is only served at certain hours), you'll be back soon just to keep an eye on your empire.

Breakfast
like royalty

65

Hash
E8

SIGNATURE DISH: Too many to pick just one

COFFEE: Locally roasted with changing weekly blends

TEA: Twinings, good old builders' or fresh mint

FOR THE MORNING AFTER: A Bloody Mary on just the right side of spicy, gin with lemonade, and made-to-order juices for the more delicate among your party

OPENING HOURS: Tuesday–Friday 8.30am–5pm; weekends 9.30am–5pm (some flexible openings over bank holidays; check Facebook for details and weekly specials)

ADDRESS: 170 Dalston Lane, E8 1NG

TELEPHONE: 020 7254 0322

NEAREST STATION: Dalston Junction, Dalston Kingsland

AWAY FROM THE MAIN HIGH STREET, HASH E8 IS ONE OF THOSE locals we all wish we had on our doorstep. But it's worth a trip even if you're not a regular Dalston hipster. Serving all the components you'd expect from a great brunch, but each has been given some deeply porky thought. The pinnacle being a towering Pig Muffin filled with all sorts of piggy delights: crisp bacon, sausage meat patty, succulent belly pork and chorizo as well as eggs, hash browns and a side of bacon jam. Phewf.

But if you're not in the mood for such porcine delights, you can treat yourself to a cheerful stack of red velvet pancakes, an outrageous French toast creation stuffed with banana, chocolate, peanut butter and dripping in maple syrup, or homemade baked beans and an omelette from the specials board. It goes without saying that ingredients are properly sourced, the bread is locally made and the pork is from a nice farm in Yorkshire. This is brunch only better and with a generous scattering of umami dust – literally, it says so on the menu. Check out their Facebook page for changing weekly dishes so you can pig-out in style.

Where
pork is king

Patty & Bun

SIGNATURE DISH: Crispy bacon, carbonara eggs and parsley mayo

COFFEE: Allpress

TEA: The usuals, but it's more about the shakes

FOR THE MORNING AFTER: Smoky Virgin Mary or a shake from the specials board

 OPENING HOURS: Brunch menu: Saturday 10am–4pm; Sunday 10am–7pm

 ADDRESS: 397 Mentmore Terrace, E8 3PH

 TELEPHONE: 020 8510 0252

 NEAREST STATION: London Fields

ON MOST BRUNCH MENUS YOU'LL FIND A BURGER HIDDEN AWAY, and you'll um and ahh to yourself, wondering if it's a bit early? NO! Not here. Patty & Bun, London Fields, says it's perfectly acceptable for your first meal of the day to be packed inside a bun (from local Pavilion Bakery on Broadway Market).

As well as the Patty & Bun regulars (which you can order from 11.30am), the brunch menu at the London Fields outpost, The Arch (in the railway arches behind the park), has a special menu of brunch buns. The crispy bacon with carbonara eggs and parsley mayo is creamy and rich with light and fluffy eggs. A meatier, more indulgent choice would be the ham collar and sausage bun, with a fresh green herb and caper salsa, oozing fried egg and melted Swiss cheese. There's also a great veggie option of fried butternut squash, spinach pesto and scrambled eggs.

There's no alcohol licence (yet) but the Smoky Virgin Mary is by no means second best – the tomatoes are smoked (on-site) making it an unexpected heady experience – and the changing shakes are outrageous. And because it's Hackney, you never know what you'll see as you leave: I saw someone ride by on a unicycle. Of course.

Brunch
in a bun!

69

Pavilion Café

SIGNATURE DISH: Pavilion Breakfast: a full English

COFFEE: Square Mile Coffee Roasters

TEA: Usuals, plus cinnamon and hibiscus

FOR THE MORNING AFTER: A creamy hot chocolate or a Camden Town Brewery beer

 OPENING HOURS: 8.30am–4pm

 ADDRESS: Corner Old Ford Road, E9 7DE

 TELEPHONE: 020 8980 0030

 NEAREST STATION: Cambridge Heath, Bethnal Green or Mile End

VICTORIA PARK OPENED IN 1845 TO PROVIDE SOME MUCH-needed green space to the built-up, overworked East Enders. Not much has changed since, and it's still a very popular place to be at the weekends – although with fewer fights at Speakers' Corner.

The café is housed in a glass pavilion next to the boating lake. There are seats inside – and a marquee in the winter – but it's best if you can nab yourself a table right on the water. From there you can see the fountains and ducks, and get some rare fresh air in the capital. It's not that near a station so it's a good destination after a walk along either the Hertford Union Canal or Regent's Canal, or up from Mile End.

The menu supports local suppliers and everything is as organic as it can get – the Ginger Pig nearby supplies the meat (and excellent black pudding) for the full Englishes, breakfast sandwiches and burgers, and the milk and other dairy comes straight from a farm on the Sussex/Kent border. The coffee is roasted less than a mile away by the Square Mile Coffee Roasters. It gets busy and there are plenty of cyclists, joggers and pushchairs, but it's a gorgeous little place to refuel before having a stroll around the restored Old English gardens.

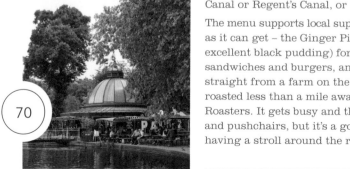

A very English breakfast in a Victorian park

Raw Duck

SIGNATURE DISH: Broken eggs

COFFEE: Caravan Market blend

TEA: Rare Tea Company or Green Tea and Roasted Rice

FOR THE MORNING AFTER: Soothing ginger and turmeric, or a drinking vinegar to aid digestion, or a breakfast cocktail

 OPENING HOURS: Weekend brunch: 10am–5pm

 ADDRESS: 197 Richmond Road, E8 3NJ

 TELEPHONE: 020 8986 6534

 NEAREST STATION: London Fields or Hackney Central

RAW DUCK FOCUSES ON SEASONAL, SIMPLE DISHES THAT AREN'T afraid to play around with strong and unusual flavours. There's definitely a Japanese influence running through the menu – and also Middle Eastern and European splashes – but the ingredients themselves are mainly wholesomely British and from excellent, reputable providers.

At the lighter end, there is homemade granola or bircher, as well as toast and house jams, but it's really the eggs cooked in myriad unusual ways that are the highlight of the day. Brown rice miso porridge with a perfectly poached egg will leave you feeling nourished and wholesome, or for something to help with a lingering hangover, the curried potatoes with salt beef and two fried eggs will give you a much-needed protein boost. But what people really go crackers for is the broken eggs, which is basically an omelette-meets-scrambled-eggs scenario with lots of umami-based flavourings and fillings – spinach and cheese, mushroom, rice and miso, or sage and anchovy.

Just down the road from London Fields, Raw Duck is the perfect little spot to while away an hour or two, sunny side up – maybe even after a dip in the lido?

Indulge in
umami

South

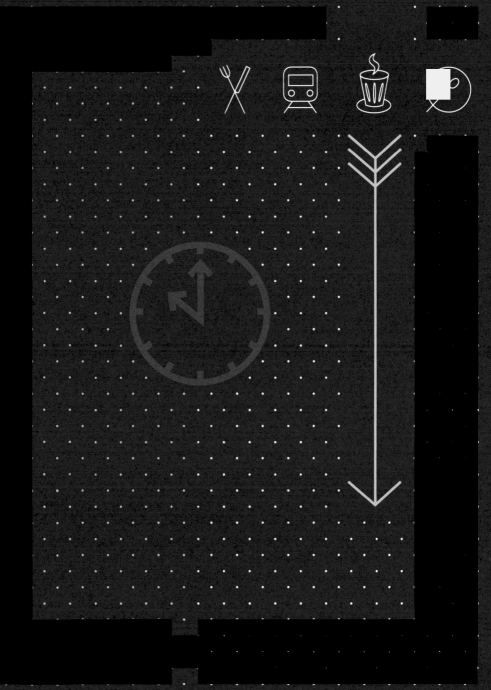

Anderson & Co.

SIGNATURE DISH:
Scrambled eggs with toppings

COFFEE: Square Mile Coffee

TEA: Birchill Teas

FOR THE MORNING AFTER:
A freshly squeezed juice

 OPENING HOURS: Weekend brunch: 9am–3pm

 ADDRESS: 139 Bellenden Road, SE15 4DH

 TELEPHONE: 020 7469 7078

 NEAREST STATION: Peckham Rye

A LOVELY, LIGHT AND BREEZY LITTLE HIDEAWAY WITH A sheltered garden in the back so you can feel like you're outside in the fresh air being wholesome, even when it's raining and you've just got out of bed. Popular with the ever-hip locals, get there early to avoid lurking in the doorway and eyeing off everyone's food. Not cool. Portions are generous, which is always welcome when you're combining two meals into one. Start with fluffy scrambled eggs on thick slices of sourdough and pile on as many toppings as you dare – perfect crispy bacon, mini chorizo, mushrooms, avocado... In place of an English muffin, go for hot potato cakes with your eggs benedict. The French toast with cinnamon sugar is thick and sweet, and there is a great cake selection at the counter. For something a little less traditionally brunchy, there are also salads and tarts of the day, and a homemade burger, the Peckhamburger.

This is a great, laid-back local that sets just the right pace for the rest of the weekend. On your way out, pick up one of the beautiful loaves of bread from the nearby bakery that fill the shelves, so you can take it home for brunch part two.

Popular in Peckham

Arlo & Moe

SIGNATURE DISH: Scrambled eggs in a multitude of guises; freshly made sausage rolls; cake!

COFFEE: Locally roasted by Dark Fluid

TEA: It's more about the coffee

FOR THE MORNING AFTER: French toast piled high with fruit and syrup

OPENING HOURS: Monday–Friday 8am–4.30pm; Saturday 9am–4pm; Sunday 10am–4pm

ADDRESS: 340 Brockley Rd, SE4 2BT

TELEPHONE: 020 3609 3151

NEAREST STATION: Croften Park or Brockley

A BROTHER AND SISTER TEAM WHO SET UP SHOP IN AN OLD barber's, Arlo & Moe is a true local favourite, giving back in supporting its fellow locals by sourcing many ingredients from the immediate area. The coffee has gained quite a following, and is brewed by nearby roaster, Dark Fluid, who only supplies his beans within a 5-mile radius. The meat inside their legendary sausage rolls is from a nearby East Dulwich butcher and all the milk, cream, butter and yoghurt are from a farm in not-all-that-far-away Kent.

It's the perfect place to people watch – from inside the big window or settled at one of the tables on the small outside terrace. Popular with local families, young children are welcome. There is a distinct 1950s feel, with mid-century furniture, pretty Formica tabletops and glass-domed cake stands displaying some delicious-looking bakes. Create your own Sexy Toast from two slices of sourdough (locally made, of course) topped with your choice from the menu, or sample one of their very moreish cakes. And make sure to grab a sausage roll before they fly off their baking trays. Oh, and don't forget to tap your foot to the great, feel-good tunes. Ah, life is OK again.

Brunch with
a vintage vibe,
and great tunes

Ben's Canteen

SIGNATURE DISH: The Big Ben

COFFEE: Allpress Coffee

TEA: Joe's Tea Co.

FOR THE MORNING AFTER: Ben's Breakfast Fizz: orange juice, marmalade syrup and Cava; or a Banging Bloody Mary

OPENING HOURS: Brunch: Friday–Sunday 9am–5pm

ADDRESS: 140 St John's Hill, SW11 1SL

TELEPHONE: 020 7228 3260

NEAREST STATION: Clapham Junction

BEN SEEMS LIKE A REALLY LOVELY GUY, AND IT'S A PLEASURE to hang out in his canteen. He said he wanted to create a pub-like vibe but that was not actually a pub, and also somewhere where you can get a really good local brunch. Well, congratulations, Ben – you did it!

Where other people may have crammed in more tables, Ben has left lots of lovely space so you never feel like you're half-involved in next-door's meal or trying to not-listen into other people's night-before gossip. There are plenty of high stools at the bar to cope with any overflow, as well as benches outside for the hardier brunchers. Food-wise there are some great all-day breakfasts including The Big Ben (well, it had to be done, really) and an egg and pulled pork dish with hollandaise, which is a little bit over-the-top, but only as the best weekend dishes should be. Another greedy option is the Breakfast Burrito – scrambled eggs and chorizo with plenty of cheese and sour cream. At the lighter and healthier end, the scrambled eggs with feta, peas and mint, or Ben's Canteen Bircher are winners all-round.

All this, and with a dog-friendly policy, I'll say that's a pretty good start to the day.

Like hanging out in a mate's pub

Brickwood Coffee & Bread

SIGNATURE DISH: Brioche French Toast

COFFEE: Caravan Market Blend

TEA: Bluebird Tea Co.

FOR THE MORNING AFTER: A cold-pressed juice

OPENING HOURS: Brunch: weekdays 7am–3pm; weekends 9am–3pm

ADDRESS: 16 Clapham Common South Side, SW4 7AB

TELEPHONE: 020 7819 9614

NEAREST STATION: Clapham Common

THERE'S A RUSTIC ANTIPODEAN FEEL TO BRICKWOOD – ALL BARE wooden boards and wall tiles – if you half-close your eyes you can almost imagine that you're in a beachside hut somewhere far away, the Indian Ocean lapping the sands outside and your surfboard propped up drying in the sun. The little courtyard in the back breaks this dream with a rather sharp bump – but it's still a nice little spot to enjoy the warmer London weather.

There are good lighter breakfast options – granola and freshly made pastries on the counter, including some gluten- and dairy-free options – and the classics are done very well: the smashed avocado is ripe and juicy and plentiful on top of a good thick slice of sourdough, with perfectly runny poached eggs and thick slices of sweet and peppery chorizo. Corn fritters seem to be ubiquitous on brunch menus at the moment, and you can sample some great specimens here, with roasted veg and beetroot crème fraiche. The brioche French toast is sweet and soft and comes with either maple banana or bacon – or both for the greedy bruncher… There are also some generously filled sandwiches (including cheese and barbecue pulled pork toasties! Could there be a more indulgent toastie pairing?!).

Leave your surfboards at the door

Burnt Toast

SIGNATURE DISH: Bread baked in-house that you can toast at your table

COFFEE: Roasted in-house

TEA: Regular builders' and the usuals

FOR THE MORNING AFTER: Full English or their well-loved pancakes, plus a Bloody Mary

 **OPENING HOURS:** Tuesday 8am–5pm; Wednesday–Friday 9am–5pm; Saturday 9am–5.30pm; Sunday 10am–5pm

 **ADDRESS:** Shop 88, Brixton Village Market, Coldharbour Lane, SW9 8PS

TELEPHONE: 07717 642812

 **NEAREST STATION:** Brixton

IN A CORNER SHOP OF BUSY BRIXTON MARKET, TAKE TIME OUT to toast freshly baked bread at the tabletop toaster to your perfect shade of golden brown. Then smother it in butter, jams and spreads. It gets busy quickly so get there early and be prepared for people in the queue to eye up your food as you eat it. But you won't be put off because it's too delicious and you can feel smug about the fact you got up earlier than them. Choose from eggs benedict, eggs and smoked salmon, a full English (or a half English, if you're not feeling so hungry) or potato rostis with various toppings, among other brunchy staples, and a feisty coffee to get you going. There's even a loyalty card for regular brunchers. The menu changes often, and the freshly baked cakes and buns inside alone are worth waiting for.

Seating is outside, under the shelter of the market, so take a cardie if you're going any time that's not summer; it's the perfect spot to watch the market bustle to life.

A toasty
brunch in
Brixton Market

Lido Café

SIGNATURE DISH: Strongman's Breakfast

COFFEE: Allpress

TEA: Lahloo

FOR THE MORNING AFTER: A cold glass of prosecco

   OPENING HOURS: Monday–Friday 9am–11.30am; weekends 9am–11.45am

ADDRESS: Brockwell Lido, Dulwich Road, SE24 0PA

TELEPHONE: 020 7737 8183

NEAREST STATION: Herne Hill or Brixton

THE CAFÉ AT BROCKWELL'S BEAUTIFUL ART DECO LIDO IS invigoratingly airy and bright. The big windows let through so much light, reflected off the water outside, that it almost seems to shimmer into the room. You can tell that the people who eat here are brimming with positivity and ambitious plans for the weekend, and maybe if you spend enough time near them, you can pick up a little of their good intentions.

Following a few brisk lengths of the pool, the gluten-free granola, packed with berries and nuts and all sorts of goodies completes a perfect wholesome start to the day. But don't worry if you fall for something a little more sinful: the Strongman's Breakfast, a really top-quality full English is all part of the training too – perfect for reloading, or whatever it is triathletes talk about. There are lots of toppings for thick slices of sourdough bread – or a gluten-free alternative – including eggs, avocado or beetroot-cured smoked salmon. And the baps are a surprise winner too. It's not often you see baps on brunch menus these days but the Lido Café's sausage or bacon baps definitely make a splash (sorry). You don't have to swim in order to eat here either – in fact, most people don't seem to – you can simply enjoy the waterside decking and catch some sunshine with a gorgeous 1930s backdrop.

A 1930s setting for a very modern brunch

Milk

SIGNATURE DISH: The Convict English muffin

COFFEE: Workshop Coffee Co.

TEA: Suki Tea

FOR THE MORNING AFTER: ¾ pint fresh fruit smoothie

 OPENING HOURS: Monday–Saturday 8am–5pm; Sunday 9am–5pm

 ADDRESS: 18–20 Bedford Hill, SW12 9RG

 TELEPHONE: 020 8772 9085

 **NEAREST STATION:** Balham or Clapham South

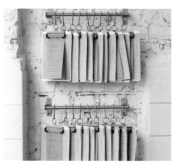

THERE'S A VERY CALMING SCANDI FEEL TO MILK WHEN YOU step inside. Cool, white and wholesome – like its namesake. Since the refurb (formally M1lk), there is also a more spacious feel, although you may be asked to share a larger table, so be prepared to bond with a new friend over your morning bacon.

A highlight of the menu is the sourdough, fresh from their nearby Brixton wood-fired ovens (the flour is from a mill in Dorset). It comes topped with eggs, every which way – including with a very special burnt-butter hollandaise. The Convict is the king of the menu though, a real head-turner of a dish: English muffin stacked with bacon, sausage, hash and an egg, which is then smothered in their own homemade 'hangover sauce' and topped with a snowy peak of cheese. It's fairly outrageous, but totally and unbelievably delicious. There are some great veggie options too including sweetcorn fritters, local Wandsworth honey dripped over homemade crumpets and, of course, fluffy buckwheat pancakes. For something a bit less bready and with a bit of a twist on a classic, try the very good baked eggs with butternut squash and feta, as well as seasonal specials. With great smoothies, even better coffee and a fun atmosphere, Milk is the perfect way to start to the day – just like our mums used to tell us.

Refreshing
and cool

MUD

SIGNATURE DISH: Breakfast Burger or Eggs Benny with belly pork

COFFEE: Ozone Coffee

TEA: We Are Tea

FOR THE MORNING AFTER: Purple juice – beetroot, apple, ginger and lime

 **OPENING HOURS:** Brunch: Monday–Friday 7am–3pm; weekends 9am–3pm

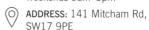 **ADDRESS:** 141 Mitcham Rd, SW17 9PE

TELEPHONE: 07889 638 261

 **NEAREST STATION:** Tooting Broadway

EVERYONE ALWAYS TALKS ABOUT THE ATMOSPHERE AT MUD and when you arrive, you'll understand why. It's just *so* friendly. It's relaxed and welcoming and the smiley staff seem only concerned with making sure you enjoy some really good food and their excellent hot coffee. Once you've secured a spot inside (beware the weekend queues) and settled onto your wooden picnic bench you won't want to go home again.

So, to the main event. The menu is short but the range of optional sides (avocado, cured salmon and housemade beans among others) just means you have an excuse to keep going back so you can find out your favourite combinations. The Breakfast Burger is enough to challenge even the hungriest, most hungover in your group – it has all the usuals – juicy pattie, bacon, cheese and a glossy egg – but with an additional surprising carby layer of potato cake. It's what you didn't even know was missing from your brioche bun.

The buckwheat pancakes are worth a very special mention too – topped with caramelised fruit and pretty edible flowers they are so comforting and such a pleasure to look at, you'll feel like you've been hugged from the inside. They are the essence of joy on a plate.

Relaxed food and great coffee

No67

SIGNATURE DISH: The Full Spanglish; their homemade beans with pepper stew is another local favourite

COFFEE: Illy

TEA: Twinings or fresh mint

FOR THE MORNING AFTER: For the health-conscious: a berry, banana and mint smoothie, and for those who are not: a Snickers milkshake

 OPENING HOURS: Breakfast: Tuesday–Friday 8.30am–11.30am; weekend brunch 10am–3.30pm

 ADDRESS: 67 Peckham Road, SE5 8UH

TELEPHONE: 020 7252 7649

NEAREST STATION: Peckham Rye or Oval, Elephant and Castle or Vauxhall and then a bus

SET INSIDE THE SOUTH LONDON GALLERY ON PECKHAM ROAD (number 67 for those in need of a helping hand with their hangovers) the dining rooms are part of the beautifully renovated Victorian house – huge windows beam in the sunlight and there's a lovely garden for alfresco eating.

A fairly broad menu covers all the breakfast staples from fruit and yoghurt, croissants and sourdough toast with a range of toppings (including their own No67 jam) to classic hot breakfasts (they do a mean bubble and squeak), sandwiches and a mezze board for sharing. Everything is done well and the dishes weave in a few twists here and there to delight your taste buds – bourbon syrup with your bacon and waffles, cured trout instead of salmon with your eggs benedict, or mushrooms cooked with white wine and thyme. Check the boards for changing seasonal specials. If you're still feeling peckish after all that, there is a tempting range of cakes for pudding – including some great vegan and gluten-free options.

When you're done, you can walk it off by taking in the latest contemporary art exhibition or browsing the bookshop.

For those who like a little art with their waffles

The London Particular

SIGNATURE DISH: The Particular Brunch Bowl

COFFEE: Higgins Coffee

TEA: Little Sparrow Tea

FOR THE MORNING AFTER: Classic Bloody Mary

 OPENING HOURS: Weekend brunch: 10am–4pm

 ADDRESS: 399 New Cross Rd, SE14 6LA

 TELEPHONE: 020 8692 6149

 NEAREST STATION: New Cross

A GORGEOUS OLD-FASHIONED KIND OF PLACE (IN THE GOOD way), but with a very modern menu, in the now *very* buzzy New Cross. Big sharing tables, both inside and out, encourage you to be sociable with your brunch, so get ready to make some new cool friends while you tuck into your eggs. But there's absolutely no pretentiousness going on here, as it's just all about the great food and even more delicious coffee.

Order The Particular Brunch Bowl with spiced Merguez sausage and all sorts of deliciously flavoured twists on the usual fry-up; with each mouthful you will feel yourself gaining power – the homemade baked beans are out of this world. As are the garlicky mushrooms – maybe not so great for inflicting on your new brunch buddies, but since most people are eating them, it's perfectly acceptable to order extra... The baked eggs are also superb and you can't beat a bacon sandwich done properly, with London Particular relish. Elsewhere, there's lots to delight any vegetarians in your group, and even the most devoted meat-lovers won't be able to resist the seasonal specials.

Laid-back local for friendly hipsters

West

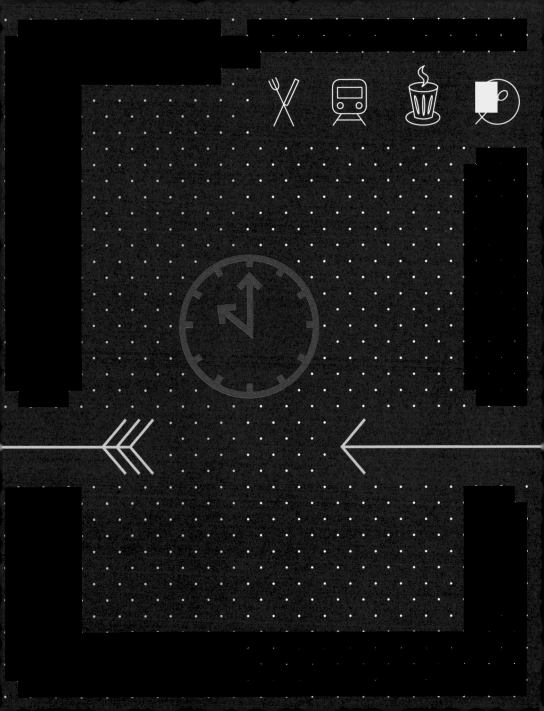

Daylesford Organic

SIGNATURE DISH: Daylesford Farmhouse Breakfast

COFFEE: Direct trade organic coffee

TEA: Loose leaf and organic

FOR THE MORNING AFTER: A Bloody Mary or a cold-pressed juice

 OPENING HOURS: Weekday breakfast: 8am–12pm; weekend brunch: Saturday 8am–5pm; Sunday 10am–6pm

 ADDRESS: 44B Pimlico Road, SW1W 8LP

TELEPHONE: 020 7881 8060

 NEAREST STATION: Sloane Square

THIS IS DEFINITELY SOMEWHERE YOU CAN TAKE YOUR PARENTS when they're visiting. It's clean and bright with lots of pot plants and a good, mostly healthy menu that you can pretend you eat all the time. As well as the lovely café there is also a deli and farmshop, selling produce delivered every day from the family farm in the Cotswolds – organic meat, veg, milk and cheese – as well as fresh bread, readymade soups and salads and sauces (plus an impressive wine list) and masses of other sustainably sourced delicacies to take home. It's a one-stop shop for the good life.

Nutty granolas and mueslis – some with mulberries, others with lots of berries – stewed fruits bircher and porridge provide the lighter brunch options, but after midday order the corned beef hash, or the smoked salmon on pumpernickel with capers and red onion. There are also plenty of eggs on toast, and the bacon roll has its own homemade brown sauce. Choose freshly baked seven-seed sourdough or from a good selection of wheat-free breads. It's a little taste of outdoor life near Sloane Square.

Fresh
from the
farm

Electric Diner

SIGNATURE DISH: Anything eggs

COFFEE: Drink one at the bar like you've just parked your truck outside

TEA: The Americans aren't famous for their tea

FOR THE MORNING AFTER: It's got to be a bourbon milkshake – it will make or break you

 OPENING HOURS: 8am–midday then an all-day menu with most of the breakfast items too

 ADDRESS: 191 Portobello Road, W11 2ED

TELEPHONE: 020 7908 9696

NEAREST STATION: Ladbroke Grove

OH, THE BACON... OH, THE WAFFLES... OH, THE RIB HASH WITH poached eggs and hollandaise! Everything on this menu is like a more exciting version of itself. The actual diner is probably not like many mid-West American diners in real life, but it's exactly like a diner in the movies – it's the diner of your dreams. Red leather booths, a long shiny counter behind which food is prepared to order by friendly staff, a soundtrack of great tunes playing over the airwaves. It is a diner that has been *electrified*.

As well as the American classics, the English breakfast is surprisingly first-rate. And although not what you might usually choose to eat in the morning, the hot dogs are some of the best dawgs in town. There's a good selection of sides, too – hash browns, macaroni and cheese, and generously thick-cut bacon. And a token healthy plate of broccoli – I wonder if anyone has actually ever ordered it... maybe it's a joke.

If you're up for celebrating greed and generally like taking things a step too far, the milkshakes will just about finish you off. The peanut butter and banana is like liquidised heaven. Or you could have pudding instead in the form of a PB & J ice-cream sandwich. Afterwards you can pop next door to the Electric Cinema to catch the latest blockbuster.

An
all-American
diner dream

DINER

Granger & Co.

SIGNATURE DISH: Broken eggs with ricotta, spinach, pine nuts and sourdough

COFFEE: Allpress

TEA: Rare Tea Company

FOR THE MORNING AFTER: Bill's Bloody Mary with clamato, wasabi, lime and coriander

 OPENING HOURS: Monday–Saturday 7am–12pm; Sunday 8am–12pm

 ADDRESS: 175 Westbourne Grove, W11 2SB

TELEPHONE: 020 7229 9111

 NEAREST STATION: Ladbroke Grove, Bayswater or Royal Oak

WHY IS IT THAT THE AUSSIES DO BRUNCH SO IMPRESSIVELY well? Laid-back and generous – both with their food and service – at Bill Granger's Notting Hill venture, brunch doesn't feel like something only for the weekend, or as a result of getting up too late for breakfast; it's a way of life.

There are, of course, plenty of health-conscious options – almond milk chia pots and house granola with coconut yoghurt and compote, and a rainbow of juices and smoothies. But even the larger dishes feel good for you. Eggs on sourdough with your choice of extra toppings is a great place to start. As well as the expected bacon, roasted tomatoes and avocado, there are some more unusual add-ons to choose from – tea-smoked salmon, miso mushrooms and a punchy salsa. In fact, most of the dishes come with some surprising flavours – the bacon and egg roll has a definite chilli hit, mellowed by mango chutney – and it's exactly what you've always wanted without even knowing it.

With windows all around the room, creating the impression the sun is permanently shining outside, and a bounty of fresh food, you will leave Granger & Co. with a healthy glow, as though you've just spent the morning outside in the great Australian fresh air.

Bill Granger
and the gang
excel again

Jackson & Rye

SIGNATURE DISH: Ribs or pancakes

COFFEE: Changing daily specials

TEA: Yes

FOR THE MORNING AFTER: Rye Mary or a Green Juice or a Leaded Shake

 OPENING HOURS: Weekend brunch menu 8am–4.30pm

 ADDRESS: 217–221 Chiswick High Road, W4 2DW

 TELEPHONE: 020 8747 1156

 NEAREST STATION: Chiswick Park or Turnham Green

UNLIKE THE 'RYE' IN SNAPS + RYE (PAGE 112), THIS RYE ISN'T referring to excellent bread, but rather excellent whisky! Possibly a bit early for hard liquor but at Jackson & Rye, as at all the Le Caprice endeavours (the Ivy, Ivy Market Grill, page 16), anything goes. The menu is long and will satisfy all and every brunch craving you could possibly imagine, from the expected bacon pancakes or avocado with eggs, to the less expected toasted marshmallows or a chargrilled whole lobster with fries. It feels a bit like you're an eccentric film star staying in an old hotel in New York or Paris and that you should order whatever you fancy right at that moment, just because you can. Even if it's an Oreo and rye milkshake at 8am. It's good ol' American food, served in generous portions, but with sophisticated old-world style.

With beautiful wooden flooring throughout and a drinks cabinet you'll wish you owned, this is definitely a place to while away some time away from reality.

Also in Soho and Richmond.

104

Catering to your every brunch-time fancy

Margaux

SIGNATURE DISH: Tartines with a range of toppings

COFFEE: Nespresso

TEA: Tea Pigs

FOR THE MORNING AFTER: Breakfast Mule or straight-up Champagne

 OPENING HOURS: Weekend brunch: 12pm–4pm

 ADDRESS: 150 / 152 Old Brompton Road, SW5 0BE

 TELEPHONE: 0207 373 5753

 NEAREST STATION: Gloucester Road or South Kensington

ELEGANT AND PARED BACK, THE DÉCOR IS AS SOPHISTICATED as the menu. There are lots of luxe copper and gold accents with sleek tabletops and spotless glassware, and the quality and style of the food lives up to its surroundings. The poached egg on toasted brioche with rich, smoky truffle mayonnaise is indulgent without being over the top, and the tartines combine flavours and textures expertly; get a few for the table and keep the bubbles flowing – the fluffy scrambled eggs with crabmeat and chives, or smoked salmon with goat's curd and avocado are generously portioned and perfectly balanced. Alternatively, opt for a more conventional starter, main, sweet format, choosing from tuna tartare, simple but well-executed salads or something hot from the grill.

The drinks list is also worth a special mention with a fabulous selection of breakfast cocktails, many with a savoury twist to offset any sweetness: a Strawberry Breeze contains a dash of balsamic, and the Breakfast Mule is beautifully bitter from grapefruit juice, aperol and vermouth.

With lots of seating – either tables for two in the busy upstairs or head downstairs for larger groups – this is a great little find on the South Ken/Chelsea border.

Unpretentious
sophistication

107

Megan's

SIGNATURE DISH: Superior Eggs Benedict

COFFEE: Fairtrade

TEA: Loose leaf

FOR THE MORNING AFTER: Passionfruit Bellini

 **OPENING HOURS:** Monday–Friday 8am–11.30am; Saturday 8.30am–3pm; Sunday 9am–3pm

 **ADDRESS:** 571 King's Road, SW6 2EB

 **TELEPHONE:** 020 7348 7139

 **NEAREST STATION:** Fulham Broadway

COSY UP INSIDE IN THE COLDER MONTHS AND FIND A SPOT IN the charming leafy courtyard when it's warmer. Tables are covered in cute little checked cloths and there's a lovely relaxed feel to the place.

The menu is a little bit haphazard and tends more towards lunch than brunch, but with a definite Mediterranean influence. Dishes range from simple eggs (the eggs benedict is, indeed, superior – it says so and it's true) to salads to sharing plates – boards of falafel, baba ganoush, grilled halloumi and meatballs, or a whole baked garlic and rosemary camembert with a pile of perfectly chewy sourdough bread.

If you're in the mood for something more substantial, choose fresh from the grill – a housemade burger or a salmon fillet with a selection from the salad bar. And the Nutella milkshake is just the right side of greedy without forcing you into needing a lie-down. For a more wholesome start to your day, go for a Green Cleanse (cucumber, spinach and apple) or Kale Greens juice (kale, cucumber, apple, mint and lemon). Both will refresh and revive even the foggiest of morning-after-the-night-before heads.

A hideaway garden in the middle of London

No. 11 Pimlico Road

SIGNATURE DISH: Breakfast sourdough bruschetta

COFFEE: Caravan

TEA: The usuals

FOR THE MORNING AFTER: Elderflower and Earl Grey Fizz

 OPENING HOURS: Breakfast: daily 9.30am–11.30am; weekend brunch 11.30am–5pm

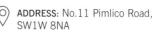 ADDRESS: No.11 Pimlico Road, SW1W 8NA

 TELEPHONE: 020 7730 6784

 NEAREST STATION: Sloane Square or Victoria

THIS IS RELAXED BRUNCHING, CHELSEA-STYLE – BRIGHT, modern and colourful with sleek marble tables and a big, well-stocked bar running along one side, and plenty of mirrors to check yourself out in. There are lots of seating options, from bigger tables and stools at the bar, to cosy nooks with comfy seats, so it's equally perfect for big groups or brunch *à deux*. It does get busy though so make sure to book ahead.

Order the breakfast bruschetta – thick slices of charred sourdough topped with roast tomatoes, spinach, avocado and beautifully crisp bacon – and a big jug of homemade lemonade for the table. Avocado on toast is taken up a notch here too in the form of a creamy cheesy toastie. And, of course, the mushrooms on toast are *truffle balsamic* mushrooms on toast – you are in SW1 after all.

There's a lighter breakfast menu to choose from, including porridge with seasonal fruits, and also a really good fruit salad – which I know sometimes seems like a bit of a cop-out, but this one is full of great flavours, like blackberries and passionfruit, and there's not a cube of honeydew melon in sight.

Afterwards, stroll down the King's Road to do some (window) shopping or get your culture fix at the nearby Saatchi gallery.

Made in Chelsea with very pretty cocktails

SIGNATURE DISH: The Full Danish or Baked Rarebit

COFFEE: Nude Espresso

TEA: Tea Pigs

FOR THE MORNING AFTER: House-infused Akvavit

OPENING HOURS: Brunch: Tuesday–Sunday all day

ADDRESS: 93 Golborne Rd, W10 5NL

TELEPHONE: 020 8964 3004

NEAREST STATION: Westbourne Park or Ladbroke Grove

SNAPS + RYE HAS A WONDERFULLY FRIENDLY ATMOSPHERE; it's as though the Danish couple who own it have personally welcomed you into their charming home – which has, as you'd expect from stylish Scandinavian design, lots of clean lines, white walls with pops of colour and calming stripped wooden floorboards. You can even buy some of the gorgeous homewares to recreate the experience in your own kitchen.

The menu pairs Nordic classics such as smørrebrød (served from midday) – a range of delicate toppings piled neatly on slices of homemade rye – with twists on British brunch staples. The Full Danish includes deliciously smoky bacon, hog's pudding, spinach and tomatoes with pickled mushrooms and their notorious Bloody Viking Ketchup. It also comes with liquorice syrup, which doesn't taste like melted Bassett's Allsorts, but rather has a deep, rich flavour that enhances all those around it. Of course, their own smoked salmon is truly excellent with eggs, as is the fresh goat's curd on rye, and there are some great pastries too.

Every dish is packed with wonderfully fresh flavour combinations that feel like contemporary versions of our usual brunch favourites.

A little
pocket of cool
Copenhagen

The Good Life Eatery

SIGNATURE DISH: Skinny Benedict

COFFEE: Hot and strong but skip it for a juice

TEA: See above

FOR THE MORNING AFTER: Ninja Turtle smoothie

 OPENING HOURS: Breakfast: Monday–Friday 7.30am–11.30am; Saturday 8am–7pm; Sunday 9am–6pm

 ADDRESS: 59 Sloane Avenue, SW3 3DH

 TELEPHONE: 020 7052 9388

NEAREST STATION: Sloane Square

THIS IS PURE HEALTH. COLD-PRESSED JUICES, ACAI SMOOTHIE bowls and chia seeds galore. But it is also seriously delicious food, in a bright and welcoming setting. The morning menu feels like room service at a luxury spa. However, because of its popularity with the hordes of local clean-eating disciples, the atmosphere is a little less than spa-like at the weekend – it's a bit of a wrestle at the counter, but hang on in there and you will be rewarded with glowing deliciousness.

If you're not up for a liquid start to the day (at least, not without a splash of the good stuff) the paleo chestnut and almond waffles or the Skinny Benedict – poached eggs with avocado and tomatoes on rye – will happily sate any hunger. OK, so there are no bacon rolls available but the frittata with almond pesto is just as umami-laden and will give you a spring in your step. I guarantee you will have glossier hair and better skin by the time you've paid the bill.

It's also food with a conscience, using locally sourced UK-based ingredients as far as possible, and working seasonally with what's available. All in all, The Good Life Eatery is where to go when you want to be a better version of yourself.

For a better,
healthier you

Tried & True

SIGNATURE DISH: T&T's Award-Winning Pulled Pork Benedict

COFFEE: Square Mile Coffee and Red Brick Espresso

TEA: Suki Tea

FOR THE MORNING AFTER: A beer from Camden Town Brewery

 **OPENING HOURS:** Breakfast: Monday–Friday 8am–4pm; weekends 8.30am–4.30pm

ADDRESS: 279 Upper Richmond Road, SW15 6SP

TELEPHONE: 020 8789 0410

NEAREST STATION: Putney

IT MAY NOT BE THE FANCIEST PLACE TO BRUNCH IN WEST London, but in every way Tried & True lives up to its name. Friendly and welcoming, you can expect no less than some very good food and – as you'd hope from any Kiwi worth his coffee grounds – a really excellent flat white every time. A sleek interior with plenty of seating, it's a relaxing place to while away a lazy weekend.

The menu fulfills all your breakfast desires – pancakes, eggs every which way, mushrooms on toast and an especially delicious bacon sandwich. But it's the pulled pork benedict that people just can't get enough of – spice-rubbed 15-hour roasted pork in a sweet and sticky sauce, shredded and served atop a beautifully light wedge of cornbread with two poached eggs and fresh chilli. It may sound as though it might be a bit much for a morning meal, but trust me when I say it isn't, and although you didn't even know it was missing from your life, once you've tasted it, you'll be back for more.

Like a home-from-home, but with better cornbread

Venues
by Postcode

CENTRAL

EC1M 5RN	Workshop Coffee Co.
EC1R 0HU	Bourne & Hollingsworth Buildings
EC1V 4JJ	The Modern Pantry
SE1 0HX	The Table
SE1 1TL	Roast
WC2E 8PS	Ivy Market Grill
WC2H 9HA	Kopapa
W1H 7NL	The Lockhart
W1T 5LZ	Honey & Co.
W1U 7PA	Chiltern Firehouse

NORTH

N1 1DA	SUNDAY
N1 5AA	Duke's Brew & Que
N1 5SB	The Towpath Café
N1C 4AA	Caravan
N4 3AJ	Boulangerie Bon Matin
N5 2LT	Fink's Salt and Sweet
N5 2XE	Franks Canteen
N8 8PL	The Haberdashery
N16 0AS	Foxlow
NW1 8UR	Greenberry Café

EAST

EC2N 4AY	Duck & Waffle
E2 7DD	Albion Café
E2 7DJ	Andina
E2 7JE	Dishoom
E2 8HZ	Beagle
E3 2PA	Counter Café
E8 1NG	Hash E8
E8 3NJ	Raw Duck
E8 3PH	Patty & Bun
E9 7DE	Pavilion Cafe

SOUTH

SE4 2BT	Arlo & Moe
SE5 8UH	No67
SE14 6LA	The London Particular
SE15 4DH	Anderson & Co.
SE24 0PA	Lido Café
SW4 7AB	Brickwood Coffee & Bread
SW9 8PS	Burnt Toast
SW11 1SL	Ben's Canteen
SW12 9RG	Milk
SW17 9PE	MUD

WEST

SW1W 8LP	Daylesford Organic
SW1W 8NA	No. 11 Pimlico Road
SW3 3DH	The Good Life Eatery
SW5 0BE	Margaux
SW6 2EB	Megan's
SW15 6SP	Tried & True
W4 2DW	Jackson & Rye
W10 5NL	Snaps + Rye
W11 2ED	Electric Diner
W11 2SB	Granger & Co.

Published in 2016 by Smith Street Books
Melbourne | Australia
smithstreetbooks.com

ISBN: 978-1-925418-02-6

CIP data is available from the National Library of Australia

Publisher: Paul McNally
Senior Editor: Lucy Heaver, Tusk studio
Design concept: Michelle Mackintosh
Design layout: Heather Menzies
Photographer: Alicia Taylor
Note: SUNDAY provided their own photography.

Printed & bound in China by C&C Offset Printing Co., Ltd.

Book 5
10 9 8 7 6 5 4 3 2 1